MW01296640

I Have Needs Too!

Supporting the child
whose sibling has special needs

Elizabeth A. Batson

Copyright © 2011 Elizabeth A. Batson

All Rights Reserved

To order copies of this book go to
http://www.DeepRootsInFrost.com/books

Thanks to the following people for their perspective on living with a sibling with special needs:

Sophie, Maddy, Deepan, Ashley, Jack, Lihi, Elena M., Shawn, Louis, Jacqueline, Ayuka, Grace, Emily, Sophia, Warren, Rajkumar, Elena M-R, Isabelle, Eliot, Gabrielle, and the other participants in the Parents Helping Parents 2010-2011 Sibling Workshops.

Deepan, Alan, Elena and Ashley also contributed drawings for this book.

Thanks also to the adults who make the sibling workshops possible: Trudy Grable, Chris Bogosian, and Maria Sinclair.

Introduction

Having a brother or sister with special needs changes a child's experience of growing up.

At the sibling workshops sponsored by Parents Helping Parents, children age 8 to 12 get a chance to talk about their experiences.

"It's hard to go out with my brother because we never know when he might throw a temper tantrum."

"I like to play with my brother. We rough-house together. But when I have a friend come over, he won't leave me alone."

"Sometimes the kids at school make fun of my sister. It is really embarrassing."

These are special children – the brothers and sisters who will be the life-long family for their sibling with special needs. They face unique challenges and they want and need their parents' support and understanding. Meanwhile, parents struggle to meet the needs of these children while coping with the extra demands of raising a child with special needs.

This book offers insight into the lives of these brothers and sisters, as well as advice on how to help them. The topics are based on the common themes that emerge in the sibling workshops: embarrassment, the wish for understanding, the sense of responsibility, the importance of fairness, the need for protection, and the love and joy that they share with their brother or sister.

Good Things & Not So Good Things
About My Brother

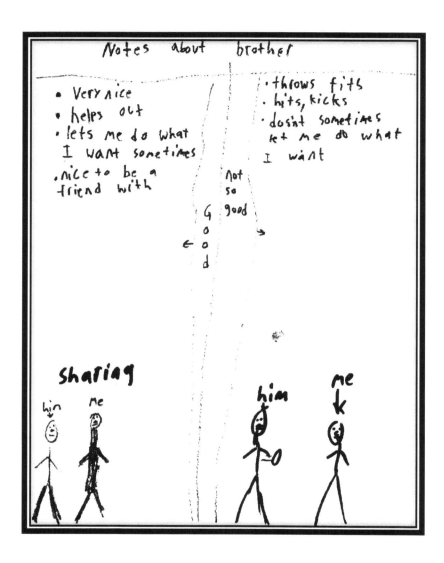

Chapter 1: Embarrassment

What it is like:

If we go to a movie, my brother wants to spend the whole time running up and down the aisle.

When we are at the grocery store, if my mother says, "No" then my brother will throw a huge tantrum and everyone will be staring at him.

Sometimes my sister will start flapping her arms. People think it is weird.

[When my brother acts up in public,] they are also looking at me because they think I might have the same thing as my brother. Even though I don't. Sometimes I feel so much embarrassment that I pretend that I'm not there.

I like to be able to talk to my parents and have them listen to my feelings. It seems strange but sometimes it helps.

I wish we could disappear when my friends say,
"Why is your brother jumping like that?"

How parents can help:

Show that you understand by summarizing the essence of what they are trying to tell you. ("You feel embarrassed when people see your sister acting like that.") Sometimes just listening and validating can be enough.

Once your child feels understood, she will be more open to hearing whatever else you want to say.

Give them in fantasy what they can't have in reality. Do they need a wall of invisibility? A mute button for their sibling? Be as silly and ridiculous as you can. This is about connecting with feelings, not taking action.

Work together to make a plan for problem situations. Having a plan gives your child a sense of control of over his own response even if he can't control his sibling.

I get embarrassed when my brother runs
up and down the aisle at the movie theater.

Embarrassment happens when you feel judged. Help your child question whether people are really judging her based on her sibling's behavior and whether she wants to accept that judgment.

If your child is being teased, teach her to ignore it or give a bland response. ("Whatever.") Tears or anger just encourages bullies. The exceptions are assault (physical violence) and theft. These are criminal actions that should be reported to the appropriate adult.

If his sibling or another child is being teased, teach your child to speak up. It might not stop the bully, but seeing someone stand up for what is right will influence the victim and bystanders.

Questioning Embarrassment

Are you embarrassed for yourself or on behalf of your sibling?

What do you think people really think when they see your sibling act that way?

Does everyone think that way?

Do your sibling's actions really say anything about who you are as a person?

Do you think those people understand the real situation or are they making assumptions?

If their judgments are based on ignorance, do you want to let that upset you?

Chapter 2: Understanding

What it is like:

I don't like to have friends come over because of my sister. There is one friend who is OK because her brother has autism too.

Sometimes when we are in the car, after school, riding home, he always talks about random things and I want some peace from him and I ask him to be quiet but my mom always sides with him. I wish she would understand that it is really hard for me. Whenever I try to tell her, she tells me just to ignore it.

I wish we could have a big sign painted outside of our house that would tell people all about autism so they would already know about it before they come inside.

How parents can help: Listen & understand

Start with reflective listening. Focus on hearing what your child is trying to tell you and then reflect back what you think you heard.

Don't tell a child what he is feeling. Use expressions like "I wonder if ..." or "In your situation, I might..."

Recognize that feelings are just a description of an internal emotional state. They are not good or bad, although they can be pleasant or uncomfortable. Accept the existence of any and all feelings in your child.

Feelings are usually mixed. Anger might cover feelings of powerlessness or guilt or sadness. Help your child notice all their different feelings and how they change over time.

There is a difference between having a feeling and acting on it. Feelings can always be accepted but we have a responsibility for how we act.

You can hear your child's feelings without having to agree with them. Listen and confirm first and then present your perspective.

Inviting your child to share with you

It sounds like you are feeling __ because __.

I wonder if you might be feeling __ as well as __?

If I were in your situation, I might be feeling ____.

I can see why you would see things that way. I see it a little differently. From my point of view, it is more about ____ than ____.

That's a tough situation. What are you going to do? *or* That's tough. Do you want some help?

How parents can help: Explaining to others

Start by helping your child understand her sibling in an age appropriate way. Learning how the disability affects her sibling's life provides a context for understanding the sibling's behavior.

Your child will look to you to see how he should react. Is this a tragedy or just a fact of life?

Don't project your worries onto your child. Children are more concerned about whether their sibling will embarrass them in front of friends than whether she will graduate from high school.

Help your child develop an age-appropriate explanation that he can use with friends.

Your child might remind her friends that their siblings can also be annoying at times. This is not unique to your family.

Friends will take their cue from your child. Help him reply so his friends can see his sibling as he does.

"Why is your sibling acting like that?"

It looks odd but it's just something he does.

She's not weird; she just has trouble keeping her body quiet when she is excited.

She has autism so she really, really likes everything to be predictable. She gets confused and scared when things change.

He has [disability]. That means his brain works differently from ours. Sometimes it's cool when he can [good attribute] but sometimes he gets frustrated and acts like that.

It's part of her having [disability] but most of the time she is a pretty good sister.

Chapter 3: Responsibility

What it is like: Responsible for sibling's behavior

When we go out, my mother tells me to make sure my brother doesn't run away but it's hard because he doesn't listen to me.

Sometimes I feel like I have to help him because I don't want him to get hurt or get sad. I always step up but then sometimes I get into trouble.

My brother is very easily annoyed. Sometimes he calls people names because they, like, push him. People start telling me like I'm responsible for his actions.

My mom says, when people come up to me and say, "Did you know that your brother did blah, blah", she always says that it is not my responsibility. She says for me to come and tell her instead of me trying to tell them.

How parents can help:

Make sure that the child is old enough and has the tools for the responsibilities they are given.

Make it clear that the adults are ultimately in charge and available if the child can't handle a situation.

Balance responsibility with freedom. Make sure your child has plenty of time to just be a child and not a caregiver.

Brother: MOM! The DVD I want is too high
Me: Shhh! I'll get it if you be quiet.

What it is like: Responsible for the feelings of others

I try to be good because I know my parents already have so much to worry about.

Sometimes my dad gets mad at me for not telling him that my brother is a problem but sometimes I am afraid because he always yells at my brother. It is hard for him to control his temper at what my brother does.

You know how most people are happy when they go on vacation? My brother HATES it. And so I want to go "whee" but I feel bad because of him.

My dad gets really mad when we don't do what we are supposed to do. He just gets really frustrated.

How parents can help

Parents set the tone of family life. Start by learning to manage your own frustration and anger. If you are struggling with this, get help.

Open up a conversation that invites your child to share his feelings. Even if you can't change things, let your child know that his feelings matter to you.

Let your child know (both in your words and behavior) that they are allowed to have problems too.

Sometimes I have to read "Toy Story"
so many times that it drives me crazy!

Inviting a conversation when the child is worried about the parents

I wonder what it was like for you when I was yelling at your brother yesterday?

It seemed to me that you looked worried when [an incident happened]. What was going on for you?

Your sister can be a handful, but that doesn't mean that you have to be perfect. Even when she has a hard day, I still care about your problems too.

I wonder if sometimes you feel like you have to be extra good to make up for all of the problems we have with your brother? [If so,] I appreciate your concern but it is important to me that you ask for help when you need me. After all, I am your parent, too.

My brother thinks it is funny when
he steps on my things.

Chapter 4: Need for Protection

What it is like:

One time my brother took a big bite out of my new toy before I even had time to play with it.

I get hurt sometimes but mostly my dad does. They try to protect my little brother from himself [as well as protecting me from him].

My brother doesn't like me listening to my iPod. When I am in my room, I always have to lock my door or he will come in and turn it off.

In one group discussion, the most common complaints were that their siblings

- *get angry very easily,*
- *wake up the whole family early in the morning,*
- *break toys, and*
- *won't leave their brother or sister alone when friends come over.*

How parents can help:

Be clear about your values. It is not OK to hurt people or destroy property.

Teach your child how to deal with her sibling on her own as well as when to ask for help.

Provide your child with a safe space for himself, if he needs it, and for his things.

Remind everyone that it is normal for siblings to have problems and also normal to love and enjoy each other.

Watching TV together

Chapter 5: Fairness

What it is like:

Sometimes I wish I had a disability too. My [older] brother gets a reward if he was good at school. I'm always good and I don't get anything.

He has to help clean up but if he doesn't, I have to clean it up all by myself.

My little brother gets whatever he wants usually. If Dad is going on an errand and he wants to come, Dad says no, he still tries to go … He just goes on until he gets what he wants … This is not fair, very frustrating.

Things my parents do right: My brother can't go to the circus, he can't go to places like that when I get to go to them and they [my parents] go with me. They do some stuff with [my brother] and some stuff with me

He's always, "I'm so tired." He's not as bad as some people with autism so I expect a little more but he doesn't help very much at all.

I got to watch the new Harry Potter with my dad alone because it was too violent for my little brother.

How parents can help:

Rule #1: Fairness is not the same as equality.

Children know this. As long as their own needs and wants are respected, they can be very understanding about the fact that their sibling gets treated differently.

All children compete for their parents' love and attention. When one child needs a great deal of attention, it can be a challenge to make sure that the other children get a turn to be the center of attention too.

Make it clear to both children that sometimes the needs of the "normal" child come first.

Find ways for your child to do things with you at his own level, even if their sibling can't handle the activity.

Schedule a "date time" to give each child a chance to do something special alone with each parent, perhaps on a weekly or monthly basis.

If your child with special needs has a positive reinforcement system, talk to your other children about whether they would like their own reward system, adjusted for their abilities.

If other children are expected to do chores, your child with special needs should have her own chores, adjusted appropriately for her age and abilities.

If certain privileges have to be earned, then the child with special needs should either not get that privilege or have their own way of earning it.

Chapter 6: Love and Play

What it is like:

Aside from everything else I kind of do like her ... no matter who says she's weird or a freak.

Sometimes I think my parents don't understand that I have deep feelings for my sister and I worry about her.

I like to play with my brother. We both like to wrestle.

When I am upset, my brother tries to make me feel better.

How parents can help:

Point out when they are enjoying each other's company.

Create opportunities for siblings to have fun together, with and without the rest of the family.

Keep the memories of the good times alive through photos and story telling. ("Remember when....")

My brother and I like to build Legos together.

Coloring or playing video games
together is fun.

Chapter 7: Final Thoughts

This book is full of advice. Feel free to pick and choose what works for you and your family.

Don't be overwhelmed. Our children don't need perfect parents. According to a leading psychologist, Donald Winnicott, children do better with the "good enough" parent. When a parent makes mistakes while still being "good enough", it teaches the child to be adaptable and independent.

Similarly, if your child gets "good enough" support, growing up with a special needs sibling is a chance to become a more compassionate, adaptable, and independent person.

About the Author

Elizabeth Batson is a registered Marriage and Family Therapy Intern (#60818) working under the supervision of Don Hadlock, LMFT (#15316) at the Process Therapy Institute in Los Gatos, California. Since August 2009, she has been counseling parents of children with special needs as well as leading the "talk circle" at monthly sibling workshops.

Previously, Elizabeth interned at the Silicon Valley Independent Living Center, counseling adults and children with disabilities.

Elizabeth has a master's degree in Counseling Psychology from Santa Clara University. She can be reached via her website at www.DeepRootsInFrost.com.

Sibling Workshops at Parents Helping Parents

Parents Helping Parents is a nonprofit in San Jose, California, dedicated to helping families with a child with special needs. For more information, visit www.php.com

PHP Sibling Workshops are for children age 8-12 whose sibling has special needs. At the workshop, these children are the center of attention: having fun and meeting other kids in a similar family situation.

Parents Helping Parents does not support or endorse any specific therapy, medication, or philosophy.

76931038R00018

Made in the USA
Middletown, DE
16 June 2018